Audrey Hepburn

A photographic journey of a beautiful

star's rise to silver-screen icon

PaRragon

Bath • New York • Cologne • Melbourne • Delhi
Hong Kong • Shenzhen • Singapore • Amsterdam

This edition published by Parragon Books Ltd in 2014
and distributed by

Parragon Inc.
440 Park Avenue South, 13th Floor
New York, NY 10016
www.parragon.com

Creative concept by The Picture Desk
All photographs from The Kobal Collection
Written by Gabrielle Mander
Designed by Beth Kalynka
Project managed by Frances Prior-Reeves
Production by Joe Xavier

ISBN 978-1-4723-5134-0

Printed in China

Introduction

Was it her fragility, her luminous beauty, poise, and talent, that took the tall, slender girl with enormous eyes, from postwar London chorus girl, model, ballet student, and bit-part starlet, to Broadway, Hollywood, and stardom? Is it because the camera, Hollywood's greatest directors, and leading men loved her; or because of the Givenchy clothes, that Audrey Hepburn, movie star, became an incandescent 20th-century icon? It was all of this, but it was her modesty, respect for others, courage, work ethic, and inner strength, that made her a great actress and a great humanitarian.

A class act

Audrey Kathleen Ruston was born in Brussels, Belgium, on May 4, 1929, to banker Joseph Ruston-Hepburn and Dutch aristocrat Baroness Ella van Heemstra, and educated in England. In Nazi-occupied Holland, during World War II, the teenage ballet student Edda (Audrey) performed in secret to raise funds for the Resistance, and carried messages hidden in her ballet shoes. She witnessed and experienced personally the horrors of war, including starvation, which affected her health and informed her life and work. In 1948, she began her career on the postwar London stage as a dancer in the chorus of the musical *High Button Shoes*; then *Sauce Tartare* in 1949; and *Sauce Piquante* in 1950.

Right: Audrey's Hollywood debut, her first Hollywood leading man, and first screen kiss. Gregory Peck, a huge star in 1953, insisted that Audrey receive top billing for her role as Princess Ann in *Roman Holiday*.

The year 1951 proved to be a watershed year for Audrey. A chance encounter, in a hotel lobby on the French Riviera, inspired French author Colette to offer Audrey the lead role in *Gigi* on the Broadway stage. With characteristic discipline and effort in rehearsal, her performance was a huge success. In 1952, she won a Theatre World Award for her role.

A star was born

Meanwhile, director William Wyler was ecstatic about her screen test for the lead role of Princess Ann in *Roman Holiday*. His confidence was justified when, in 1954, Audrey won the Academy Award for Best Actress in her first Hollywood movie. A star was born.

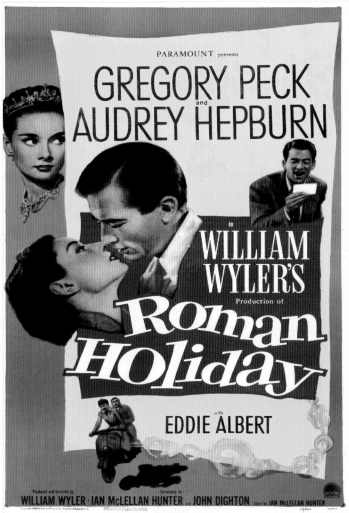

Top: Colette with her perfect Gigi. Audrey's unusual beauty was Colette's ideal for her creation, the gamine Gigi. Fortunately, Audrey could sing, dance, and act too.

Opposite: From chorus girl to lead: Audrey made the role of Gigi her own, in Anita Loos' adaptation of *Gigi*.

Bottom: Established star Gregory Peck's gracious support allowed Audrey to "steal" the film *Roman Holiday*.

Audrey's apparent meteoric rise to stardom belied her self-sacrifice and determination. She worked tirelessly on her acting technique for *Gigi* and she had extraordinary charisma. As Anita Loos remarked, "She seemed to have a line drawn around her, the way only children have. Whatever she did, she stood out." This was equally and strikingly evident as a loving mother to two sons and in her tremendous work as ambassador for UNICEF.

Cinderella syndrome?

After Audrey's Oscar-winning movie debut as Princess Ann in *Roman Holiday*, starring roles flooded in, until her virtual retirement in 1967 following her virtuoso performance in *Wait Until Dark*. Highlights of her career include the modern Cinderella in *Sabrina* (1954), a Russian noblewoman in *War and Peace* (1956), and a fashion Cinderella in *Funny Face* (1957). In 1959, she gave a subtle, critically acclaimed performance as Sister Luke in *The Nun's Story*, and switched to kooky party girl in *Breakfast at Tiffany's* in 1961. In 1963, she charmed audiences as an unwitting Parisian gangster's moll in *Charade*, and *My Fair Lady* (1964) saw her as Cinderella (again). Audrey Hepburn lived and acted "from the inside out"—with integrity. She gave unstintingly to her directors and, until her death in 1993, caring for starving children. Her ravishing beauty lives on.

Opposite: This 1954 portrait is a perfect example of Audrey's timeless beauty, although her look was considered unconventional at the time. She seems unconsciously alluring, yet naive; poised, yet vulnerable. She resisted Hollywood's demand to pluck her thick dark eyebrows, her complexion is flawless, and her huge eyes and bone structure are incredible.

Top: A 1953 portrait of Audrey by distinguished Hollywood studio photographer Bud Fraker. Audrey had already modeled in London before her movie career began, and the combination of her elfin beauty and Fraker's skill with the camera resulted in a masterpiece.

Bottom: This beautiful portrait of Audrey was taken in 1954, after she had already won an Academy Award for *Roman Holiday* and had appeared as a water sprite in *Ondine* on Broadway with Mel Ferrer, for which she won a Tony award. She fell in love with and married her costar that year, which perhaps accounts for her soft smile and unmistakable allure in this photograph.

Opposite: Another beautiful photograph of Audrey, taken by Bud Fraker: a publicity still for *Sabrina* in which he has captured the wistfulness in her eyes, a sense of young love unrequited. This was the very quality that she brought to the part, as the teenager in love with a wealthy playboy who hadn't noticed that she existed. She and costar William Holden had a passionate affair during filming.

Left: The year 1954 continued to be an outstanding year for Audrey, and she and photographer Bud Fraker were an unbeatable partnership, as this picture shows. It is very rare to find a less than perfect picture of Audrey, but Fraker manages to capture every nuance of expression in her matchless face.

Opposite: In *Funny Face,* Audrey plays Jo Stockton, the intellectual assistant in a Greenwich Village bookstore who is transformed into *Quality* magazine's "Quality Woman," "full of grace, elegance, and pizazz." This 1956 studio portrait, taken for the movie, shows beauty and intelligence as well. The character of the photographer, played by Fred Astaire, was based on famous fashion photographer Richard Avedon, who advised on the photographs in the production.

Laughter in Paradise

Audrey was dancing in the London revue *Sauce Piquante* when she was noticed and invited to make her British screen debut. A tiny part in *One Wild Oat* was followed by this 1951 comedy caper from Mario Zampi. Although she played only a small part—Frieda, the cigarette girl—she was in exalted company. The movie starred the British actor, Hugh Griffith, as eccentric millionaire and practical joker Henry Russell, who leaves his fortune to his four heirs—played by Fay Compton, Guy Middleton, George Cole, and Alastair Sim—but with strings attached.

Here comes the bride

Before they can get their hands on the money, each must, within one month, successfully face a challenge alien to their characters. Reluctant Simon Russell (Guy Middleton) must marry, and, unaccountably, he is less than eager to make Frieda his bride.

Right: Audrey looks spectacular in *Laughter in Paradise*. When director Zampi saw how she lit up the screen, it is said that he saw her potential and increased her screen time at once.

THE Lavender Hill Mob

Once again, Audrey joined a distinguished cast, headed by Alec Guinness and Stanley Holloway, in this, her third feature film of 1951. *The Lavender Hill Mob* is now known as a legendary "Ealing Comedy," produced by Michael Balcon for Ealing Studios in West London, and directed by Charles Crichton. Its original screenplay won an Oscar for writer T. E. B. Clark.

One liner

Although Audrey speaks only a little of his award-winning dialogue, she was making progress in her movie career and looked sensational in the small part of Chiquita. Alec Guinness as Holland (previously a virtuous bank clerk), and Stanley Holloway (playing a souvenir maker), team up in this caper, to plan and execute a gold bullion heist and export the loot in the form of models of the Eiffel Tower, assisted by Sid James and Alfie Bass as crooks Lackery and Shorty, respectively.

Left: Producer Michael Balcon is said to have bitterly regretted not signing Audrey to a contract. *The Lavender Hill Mob* was a box-office hit, and Audrey, seen here with Alec Guinness and William Fox, was definitely "noticed."

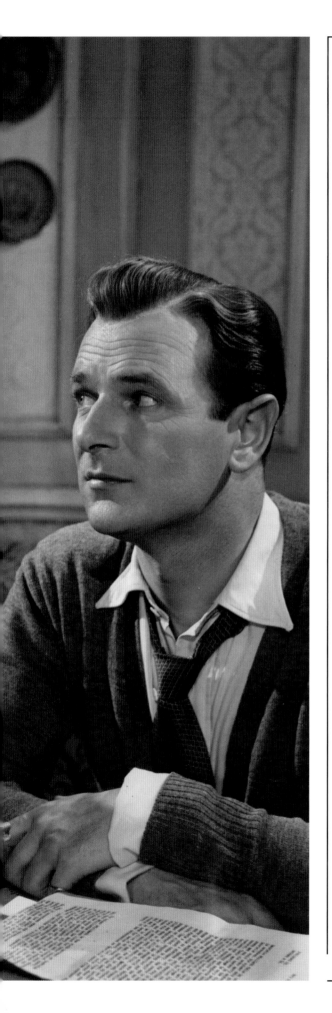

Young Wives' Tale

Still in 1951, Audrey extended her repertoire with this farce, starring Nigel Patrick and Joan Greenwood as Rodney and Sabina Pennant, one of two couples who are victims of a postwar housing crisis in London and a shortage of reliable child care, forcing them to share living space. Confusion and misunderstandings abound, as the characters pop in and out of the suburban home in which all the action takes place.

And what a tale …

This was the tagline for the movie, and Eve Lester (Audrey Hepburn) has a part to play, albeit a small one. She becomes entangled with Rodney in one of the picture's many plot twists and apparent affairs.

Left: Eve Lester and Rodney Pennant share a scene. Audrey is said to have described herself as director Henry Cass's "whipping boy" on this movie. Unusually for Audrey, she seemed unable to please the director, recalling that nothing she did seemed good enough.

Secret People

This 1952 movie was one of Thorold Dickinson's last as a director, and Audrey's first drama. *Secret People* starred Valentina Cortese as Maria Brentano, a woman who has escaped a fictional European dictatorship after her father was murdered. She flees with her younger sister Nora (Audrey Hepburn) to 1930s England. Seven years later Maria encounters her former lover, who embroils the sisters in a plot to assassinate the dictator. An innocent bystander is killed.

I'm a dancer

Audrey's experience strengthened with each movie she made, and although this was a supporting role it gave her an opportunity to extend her range and to use her extensive training in her first love—ballet. She had studied with the Ballet Rambert after the war, but had grown too tall to be a prima ballerina. Her dance background was evident in her grace and poise, and broadened the scope of the roles she might be offered.

Right: Audrey's balletic dream is fulfilled. She had the talent and training, and although she was too tall to work with principal male dancers on stage, this was not an issue on film.

Opposite: A girlish Audrey (Nora) at the barre sees her reflection, highlighting the psychology of the movie's subtext: that each of us has a "secret person" inside and we are not aware of what we might each be capable. Valentina Cortese requested that Audrey be given the part, after seeing her at an audition for ballerinas, and became something of a mentor to the young actress.

Off the record

Above: Could Audrey have imagined, in 1952, that she would be rubbing shoulders with legendary composers and lyricists Irving Berlin and Cole Porter? Yet here she is in 1953, looking composed and happy, celebrating her first Hollywood feature, *Roman Holiday*.

Opposite: Audrey had some very interesting costumes, from tomboyish teen to Parisian couture, for the movie *Sabrina*. Here, in an off-set shot, but still in her car washing costume, she is relaxing, like any lovesick young woman in 1954, with a phonograph and a stack of love songs.

Top left: *Sabrina* saw Audrey's character, Sabrina Fairchild, transfer her unrequited infatuation with David Larrabee to his brother Linus (Humphrey Bogart). Bogart is said to have been unimpressed with the casting of Audrey as Sabrina. By the time the movie wrapped, he had shaken Audrey's hand and admitted that he had been wrong. Here the young star chats with Hollywood legends "Bogey" and Marlene Dietrich.

Bottom left: The beautiful, elaborate costumes that fashion photographer and designer Cecil Beaton devised for *My Fair Lady* took both filmgoers' and critics' breath away. By 1964, Audrey was a star many times over, and here we see her with costar Rex Harrison, dressed for the pivotal ballroom scene. The semireclining chairs enabled them to relax between takes without damaging their sensational costumes.

Love and Marriage

Opposite top: Audrey Hepburn and Mel Ferrer were married in 1954 in a simple ceremony in Bürgenstock, Switzerland, near their home. Audrey wore an elegant, white organdie gown by Balmain, with a simple wreath of roses in her hair. In 1953, she had been engaged to James Hanson, but called off the wedding when it became clear that their demanding careers were keeping them apart. She said, "When I get married, I want to be *really* married."

Left: Audrey and husband Mel relaxing at home in 1955. Since their marriage, Audrey's schedule had been frantic and sadly, as a result, she suffered the first of several miscarriages. As a very private person, she kept her heartbreak to herself, working tirelessly.

Opposite bottom: Audrey Hepburn, Mel Ferrer, and their longed-for first child, four-year-old Sean, face reporters in 1964. By this time, the Ferrer marriage was showing signs of strain, although Audrey, who had been much affected by the breakup of her parents' marriage and her father's absence, was determined to keep the family together. Friends believed Mel Ferrer to be a controlling force in both Audrey's career and their private life. They finally divorced in 1968.

Roman Holiday

Young Princess Ann leads a life circumscribed by duty and an aged court. Where better than 1950s Rome, the natural home of the paparazzi, to escape and experience the life that other young people enjoy? Sneaking out, she embarks on a romantic Roman holiday with reporter Joe, unaware of his professional interest.

"Over here, Audrey!"

Audrey was chosen to star as director William Wyler's princess, despite her inexperience. Wyler, leading man and major star Gregory Peck, and legendary costume designer Edith Head, fell in love with her dignity, vulnerability, and honesty in a short interview at the end of her gorgeous screen test.

Right: Under the influence of a sedative taken before leaving her embassy, Ann finds herself alone in the rooms of American journalist Joe. Fortunately, her naive vulnerability touches the hard-bitten reporter. Both Peck and Hepburn denied rumors of romance, though Audrey added, "Actually, you have to be a little bit in love with your leading man and vice versa. If you're going to portray love, you have to feel it. You can't do it any other way. But you don't carry it beyond the set."

Opposite: *Roman Holiday* was shot on location in Rome and captured the spirit of 1950s modernity, optimism, and style, set against the background of the eternal city. The scooter was the perfect way to see the sights and avoid traffic and became the trademark of Italian youth.

William Wyler's confidence in Audrey's ability to play Princess Ann in *Roman Holiday* was not misplaced. As well as the Academy Award for Best Actress, she won a BAFTA for Best British Actress, and a Golden Globe. Paramount signed her to a seven-picture contract: and the critics…?

Elfin and wistful

The *New York Times*' A. H. Weiler wrote:
"Although she is not precisely a newcomer to films Audrey Hepburn, the British actress who is being starred for the first time as Princess Ann, is a slender, elfin and wistful beauty, alternately regal and childlike in her profound appreciation of newly found, simple pleasures and love…"

Opposite: Princess Ann rejoices in an illicit haircut. Her classic, long locks are shorn by a reluctant Roman barber, who invites her to go dancing when he inspects his handiwork. The "Audrey look" became all the rage after her image appeared on the cover of *TIME* magazine.

Left: The beautiful Princess in regal mode, with a touch of rueful mischief. The *New York Times* continued, "…Although she bravely smiles her acknowledgment of the end of that affair, she remains a pitifully lonely figure facing a stuffy future." Part of the popularity of the movie was attributed to the public's interest in the beautiful, real-life English princess, Princess Margaret, and her struggle to marry a divorced commoner, Group Captain Peter Townsend.

Audrey really was already a consummate actress, even in her first Hollywood part. During her apprenticeship, playing bit parts in the famous Ealing Comedies, she had had plenty of time to study the techniques of great comedy actors like Alastair Sim and Alec Guinness. Her dramatic performance was sensitive and intelligent and she had real life to call upon for romantic scenes.

Crocodile tears

William Wyler said that his only difficulty was in getting her to shed tears. As Gregory Peck recalled, "Here was a girl good at everything but shedding tears … when it came to the poignant scene, Wyler had to scare the wits out of her." Perhaps the teenager who survived Nazi-occupied Holland had shed enough real tears to last a lifetime?

Right: Many American and British soldiers had served in war-torn Italy during World War II. It was uplifting for postwar audiences to see the chic, vibrant capital and the optimism of youth in liberated 1950s Europe. In this shot, Joe Bradley (Gregory Peck), Princess Ann (Audrey Hepburn), and photographer Irving Radovich (Eddie Albert) avoid trouble during Ann's Roman holiday.

Sabrina

A colossal year for Audrey was 1954; after the success of *Roman Holiday*, Paramount cast her in another romantic comedy. This time she played the eponymous heroine of director Billy Wilder's *Sabrina*. This rags to riches story concerns the chauffeur's daughter and her hopeless teen passion for David Larrabee (William Holden), the playboy younger brother of Linus (Humphrey Bogart), the hardworking bachelor head of the family.

May to December

After her transformation in Paris, David finally notices Sabrina. Linus attempts to break up their romance in favor of an advantageous, arranged marriage for David, and ends by falling for the bewitching Sabrina himself.

Opposite: Sabrina at last catches the eye of playboy David Larrabee. At twenty-five, Audrey could play both the teenage and the adult Sabrina convincingly. The real-life romance between Hepburn and Holden, who was thirty-six, is more plausible than the movie plot, in which she falls instead for Humphrey Bogart, thirty years her senior.

Top: This stunning Bud Fraker studio shot shows the difference that a sojourn in Paris can make to a young lady in pursuit of love. Sabrina's ballgown, designed by Hubert de Givenchy (who henceforth designed all Audrey's clothes) completed her transformation—it was the first of many professional and personal collaborations between the star and the couturier.

Bottom: This illustration for a lobby card/poster hardly does justice to Audrey's exceptional beauty. She has made her way up the billing since *Roman Holiday*, but naturally Bogart has the top spot in this Billy Wilder romantic comedy.

HUMPHREY
BOGART
AUDREY
HEPBURN
WILLIAM
HOLDEN

"SABRINA"

with
WALTER HAMPDEN · JOHN WILLIAMS · MARTHA HYER · JOAN VOHS
PRODUCED AND DIRECTED BY
BILLY WILDER
Written for the Screen by BILLY WILDER, SAMUEL TAYLOR and ERNEST LEHM From the play by SAMUEL TAYLOR A Paramount Picture

War and Peace

War and Peace (1956) is a sumptuous adaptation of Tolstoy's masterpiece: a story of love and conflict in two noble Russian families, during Napoleon's 1812 campaign. Newlyweds Ferrer and Hepburn wanted to make the movie together.

Wishing on a star

Audrey had signed to star as Natasha Rostova when she asked producer Carlo Ponti to cast her husband as Prince Andrei. Although Ferrer was a fine and sensitive actor, his star was waning; Audrey's was in the stratosphere. In the event, he gave a fine performance, and Audrey was flawless. Alas, the movie didn't set the box office on fire.

Below: Audrey, ravishing as ever as Natasha Rostova, hadn't ridden since childhood; most of the riding in the movie was done by stunt doubles or on mechanical horses. Four years later, Audrey was to break her back when she fell from a horse while filming *The Unforgiven*.

Opposite: This poster for King Vidor's *War and Peace* shows Audrey as Natasha flanked by her costars. Henry Fonda at fifty was miscast as Pierre; Audrey had lobbied for her *Roman Holiday* costar, Gregory Peck, to play the role.

Funny Face

Funny Face (1957) is the story of a young intellectual's metamorphosis into a fashion model for *Quality* magazine. Shot on location in Paris, with costumes sketched by Givenchy, some songs by George and Ira Gershwin, stills photography by Richard Avedon, and dancing by Fred Astaire, *Funny Face* is gorgeous to look at. An incandescent Audrey stars as Jo Stockton, with Kay Thompson as the fabulous editor of *Quality* magazine.

All singing, all dancing

Stanley Donen directs a fun, witty satire, showcasing Audrey's talents as a dancer, singer, and actress. She feared that she wouldn't dance well enough to partner Astaire. She said, "I have waited twenty-seven years to dance with Fred Astaire at last."

Opposite: This stunning picture, from an imaginary fashion shoot, was taken by world-famous fashion photographer, Richard Avedon. Astaire's character, Dick Avery, is loosely based on Avedon, who designed the opening sequence and was an adviser on the movie.

Below: In this scene still, Dick coaxes Jo's imagination. Astaire is fabulous, though thirty years Audrey's senior, as is the backdrop of Paris in the rain, allowing Audrey to shine as a model and an actress.

Kay Thompson's performance as the fierce, professional, uncompromising fashion editor in *Funny Face* is one of the movie's highlights. She rarely appeared on screen, preferring musical direction. Her character was allegedly based on the fabled *Vogue* editor, Diana Vreeland. As always, Astaire's performance was brilliant and flawless.

"Something old, something new."

"Something old, something new" was how one critic described the movie, and at fifty-eight, Astaire joked that he was the "something old." Audrey brought style, zest, beauty, energy, and youth to the picture. Her touching rendition of "How long has this been going on?" is her first musical performance on screen.

Right: Off set with Audrey's personal couturier, Hubert de Givenchy. Many people attributed the iconic, simple elegance of the "Audrey look," both on and off screen, to her impeccable taste, slender figure, and his clothes.

Top: In this poster for a movie in which high fashion couture is the third star, Audrey is featured in her least glamorous costume. The simple, effective black outfit appears in the Bohemian modern-dance sequence, which she performs in the "empathacalist" nightclub.

Bottom: "Never work with children or animals" is an old acting adage. Audrey was always perfectly at home with both, and looks perfectly beautiful in this shot. The wardrobe mistress complimented Hepburn's charm, patience, and professional attitude during the many costume changes that the screenplay required.

Love in the Afternoon

Love in the Afternoon (1957) saw Audrey reunited with director Billy Wilder and back in Paris on location. Ariane Chavasse (Audrey Hepburn) overhears her private investigator father's client threaten to kill his wife's lover, player Frank Flanagan (Gary Cooper). Innocent Ariane warns Frank, and as they become involved Ariane pretends to be a femme fatale. Intrigued, Frank employs her father to investigate her "past."

May to December (again)

Hepburn's, Cooper's, and Maurice Chevalier's performances, and the movie itself, received great reviews; the *New York Times* called it "… a grandly sophisticated romance" but the age difference between Hepburn and Cooper (who was fifty-five) left some audiences feeling incredulous about the plot.

Right: The real Ariane is an innocent dreamer, as this photograph shows.

Opposite top: The picture of innocence, Ariane is the charming music student who meets her lover for a picnic in the afternoon. Chevalier and Audrey became close friends on this movie. He sent flowers to her mother, saying, "To her real mother from her reel father."

Opposite bottom: Ariane the femme fatale. Frank calls Ariane "Thin girl" in the movie. Wilder said of Hepburn, "Off camera, she was just an actress. She was very thin, a good person, sometimes standing on the set she disappeared. But (when she stood before the camera) there was something … just absolutely adorable about her. You trusted her."

Green Mansions

Rima the Bird Girl (Audrey Hepburn) is an orphan living in the Amazonian jungle. She befriends a young Venezuelan, Abel (Anthony Perkins), who has fled revolution in his native land. In 1959, Mel Ferrer directed his wife in this lavishly photographed but critically panned movie. Audrey was perfect casting for the otherworldly Rima.

First and last

Sadly, Ferrer's direction of Dorothy Kingsley's adaptation of the William Henry Hudson novel disappointed the critics. Ferrer had intended *Green Mansions* to be the first of a number of movies starring his wife and directed by him, but this was the first and only one released.

Opposite: Anthony Perkins and Audrey Hepburn appear as Abel and Rima in this scene still from *Green Mansions*. Audrey was anxious to support her husband and to spend as much time together as their conflicting schedules would allow. She was bewitching in the role, but the movie was not a success.

Right: Audrey wanted this collaboration with her husband to be a success, and she brought much charm as well as her trademark elfin mystique to the role. Privately, by 1959 she was more eager for the Ferrers to collaborate in starting a family.

The Nun's Story

Fred Zinnemann directed this powerful and hugely successful 1959 movie, based on a true story. Gabrielle Van Der Mal (Hepburn), the daughter of a brilliant Belgian surgeon, enters the convent with a vocation to nurse the sick in the Belgian Congo. She becomes Novice Sister Luke and struggles with her vows of humility and obedience.

War and peace

Eventually she is sent to the Congo, where her association with the brilliant but atheist Dr. Fortunati (Peter Finch) challenges her faith and, it is implied, her vow of chastity. On her return to Belgium she finds it impossible to accept the horrors of the Nazi occupation, and the murder of her father.

Opposite: Audrey Hepburn looked extraordinarily beautiful in the full habit of a nun. She met Marie Louise Habets, the nun on whose life the story was based, while preparing for the part, and Marie Louise helped nurse Audrey when she suffered a serious accident during the filming of *The Unforgiven*.

Top: In this still, Sister Luke's passion and intelligence are evident in her face as the novice struggles with her vows. Audrey had her own tragic experience of living under Nazi occupation to inform her work.

Bottom: Sister Luke and Dr. Fortunati find a grudging respect and admiration for one another, despite their spiritual differences. Audrey often cited this movie as her favorite.

The Great and the Good

Top: Audrey Hepburn and Fred Astaire chatting off set on location for *Funny Face* in 1956. Audrey was always a dancer at heart and was prepared, as always, to work tremendously hard to meet Astaire's exacting standards. He loved and respected her in return. She was characteristically modest: "I was asked to act when I couldn't act. I was asked to sing in *Funny Face* when I couldn't sing, and dance with Fred Astaire when I couldn't dance—and do all kinds of things I wasn't prepared for. Then I tried like mad to cope with it."

Bottom: Audrey Hepburn with two of Hollywood's most respected directors, Billy Wilder and William Wyler. Both men adored and admired her and welcomed her as a breath of fresh air in Hollywood. Wilder said, "Audrey Hepburn, singlehanded, may make bosoms a thing of the past. Never again will a director have to invent shots where the girl leans forward for a scotch and soda." Wyler added, "After so many drive-in waitresses becoming movie stars … along comes class … it's a rare quality, but boy do you know when you've found it."

Opposite: Audrey Hepburn and William Holden in 1956. Audrey and Bill remained good friends after their love affair ended when *Sabrina* (1954), the first movie they made together, wrapped. They starred together again a decade later, in *Paris When it Sizzles* (1964). The mature rapport between them enhanced this "screwball comedy."

The Unforgiven

In 1960, Audrey appeared with two Hollywood legends, Burt Lancaster and Audie Murphy, in her first western, directed by John Huston. Both she and Huston jumped at the script, a tale of racial intolerance in a Texas frontier town, when the Zachary family discover that their "sister" Rachel is, in fact, a Kiowa Indian, stolen at birth. Huston lost faith with the movie when he was forced to make a swashbuckler rather than the subtle social commentary he had planned.

Riding for a fall

Audrey was determined to do her own riding and, in her rest periods, she practiced riding bareback while managing her long skirts. Her horse, aptly named Diablo, was spooked and threw her. She broke her back.

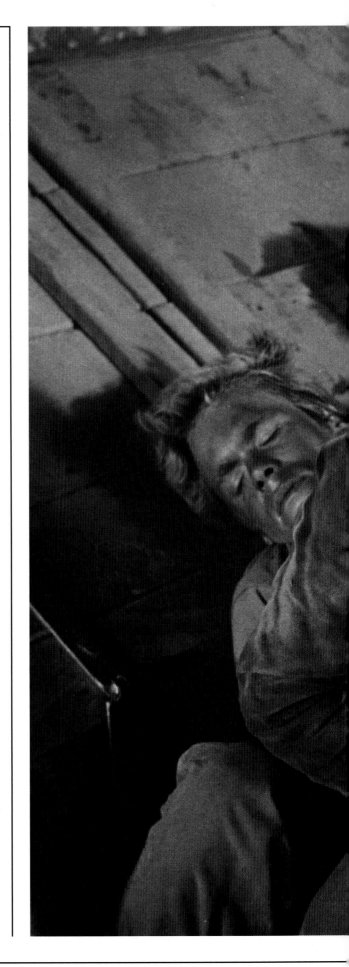

Right: Rachel (Audrey Hepburn) must fight against her tribe and, in doing so, she must make a heartbreaking choice between the Kiowa and her adoptive family. Audrey looked beautiful and acted convincingly, but her accent was not as perfect as her face.

Inset: Poster for *The Unforgiven* (1960). Lancaster, Huston, and Hepburn should have been a dream team, but artistic difficulties and ill fortune dogged the production. When Diablo threw Audrey, her heart as well as her back was broken, when she miscarried for the second time.

Breakfast at Tiffany's

In 1961, Blake Edwards directed the movie that would confirm Audrey's iconic star status forever. Costarring George Peppard as reluctant gigolo Paul Varjak, and with a controversial performance from Mickey Rooney as Mr. Yunioshi, *Breakfast at Tiffany's* captures the zeitgeist of a world on the cusp of the 1960s.

"... A no-name slob"

Although the hard edges of Truman Capote's novella were softened for the screenplay, the movie remains remarkably true to the book, and Audrey conveyed impeccably the duality of the dirt-poor, backwoods child bride reinvented in the New York sophisticate.

Right: Holly Golightly enjoys a pastry and takeout coffee in the early hours of the morning. The "Audrey look," established with *Roman Holiday*, developed in *Sabrina* and *Funny Face*, was perfected in *Breakfast at Tiffany's*.

Opposite top: Standing out in a crowd was never a problem for Audrey, nor indeed Holly. Even dressed in a sheet, Audrey's beauty and sophisticated sex appeal are undeniable.

Opposite bottom: Audrey Hepburn posing with Henry Mancini. Audrey worked with great composers, directors, and actors throughout her career. Mancini said that he wrote the melody of "Moon River" to suit Audrey's singing voice, accompanied by an acoustic guitar.

The enduring epitome of style: Givenchy's iconic "little black dress," Oliver Goldsmith's enormous sunglasses, and an overlong cigarette holder defined Holly Golightly as a 1961, uptown, Manhattan party girl. But it is Hepburn's sensitive portrayal of the beautiful, naive, fragile, kooky Holly—a girl prepared to sacrifice both love and "Cat" for the kind of financial security that only Tiffany represents—that has captivated audiences for over half a century.

Crossing it with style

Author Truman Capote wanted Marilyn Monroe for the part, but it was Audrey's performance, Blake Edwards' direction, and Henry Mancini's Oscar-winning score that combined to make classic cinema.

Opposite: Chic yet mischievous: the iconic Holly.

Top: Holly introduces Paul to her secret passion, Tiffany. Blake Edwards had some difficulty in clearing the corner of New York's Fifth Avenue and 57th Street to shoot the location scenes.

Bottom: Beautiful and vulnerable, Holly turns "Cat" out into the rain, symbolizing her rejection of commitment.

The Children's Hour

William Wyler directed Audrey once again in the courageous drama *The Children's Hour* (1961), based on a play by Lillian Hellman. College friends, Karen Wright (Audrey Hepburn) and Martha Dobie (Shirley MacLaine) have cofounded a small boarding school for girls in an idyllic American town. Karen is engaged to local doctor Joe Cardin (James Garner), and the school is becoming well established.

Seeds of doubt

In the course of disciplining a duplicitous child, Mary, the seeds are sown for the collapse of Karen and Martha's world. Spiteful Mary whispers a lie, a tale of lesbianism between her teachers, which both rocks the foundations of the school and poisons the relationships between Karen, Joe, and Martha.

Right: Audrey Hepburn, as Karen Wright, fears for her life as witch hunting in a small town takes on a new meaning. It was exceptionally courageous of Audrey, who had always guarded her screen image so carefully, to take the part of Karen Wright. Wyler's masterly casting and direction, superb performances from the entire cast, and the strength of the screenplay, took the movie's themes of latent lesbianism, prejudice, and fear to mainstream audiences: a major feat for 1961.

Opposite: Audrey's 1960s glamour, as seen in this contemporary studio portrait, was of necessity more subdued on screen for her role as Karen Wright.

Charade

In 1963, cinema audiences were treated to *Charade*, a motion picture that brought together the dream team: Stanley Donen directed and Audrey Hepburn starred with Cary Grant, Walter Matthau, and a stellar supporting cast, in a screwball/thriller/romance, filmed in Paris, with music by Henry Mancini.

Expect the unexpected

Reggie Lampert (Hepburn) becomes entangled with Peter Joshua (Grant) when her husband is murdered and revealed to be in possession of several passports, a ticket to Venezuela, and a letter addressed to his wife. A complex plot and witty banter ensue. Reggie pursues Peter, since Cary Grant was concerned that the twenty-six-year age difference between the stars would make his pursuit of her unseemly.

Top: Audrey is pursued through the Paris Metro by both Grant and Matthau. Whom should she trust? Off set, she was delighted to be in Paris, near to her much longed-for son, Sean, who had been born in 1960.

Bottom: *Charade* surpassed the promise made in the poster, with fast-paced action and countless plot twists.

Opposite: In the 1960s, Audrey and Brigitte Bardot were responsible for making the trench coat, with loosely tied belt and a headscarf, an iconic fashion look—dark glasses are essential.

CARY Audrey
Grant Hepburn

You can expect the unexpected when they play...

"Charade"

a STANLEY DONEN production in TECHNICOLOR®

co-starring
WALTER MATTHAU James Coburn Screenplay by PETER STONE
Produced and Directed by STANLEY DONEN Music HENRY MANCINI A UNIVERSAL RELEASE

UNIVERSAL CITY STUDIOS

Paris When It Sizzles

This movie, released in 1964, was shot in 1962 on location in Paris, back to back with *Charade*. It stars William Holden as Audrey's leading man, a playboy writer too busy drinking to write the script that his boss (Noël Coward) is expecting in two days' time. She is the typist in his hotel room, with nothing to type, to whom he looks for inspiration.

Sizzling rumors

The gossip columns were agog to know if the stars would rekindle the affair that they enjoyed on *Sabrina*. Holden had loved Audrey ever since, but she was now married and not interested. The movie has some interesting cameo appearances too.

Opposite: Starring the Eiffel Tower, Paris was the perfect backdrop for this kooky romantic comedy. Audrey and William Holden are caught in a moment between scenes.

Left: Audrey seemed only to become more beautiful with the passing of time, despite her private sorrows. At last, she and husband Mel Ferrer had their son, and Audrey believed in her marriage vows, but despite her efforts, her marriage was disintegrating.

My Fair Lady

Audrey was thrilled to be offered the role of Eliza Doolittle in George Cukor's *My Fair Lady* (1964). The stage musical, adapted from George Bernard Shaw's *Pygmalion*, starring Julie Andrews, had been a triumph. Audrey had loved it and longed to play Eliza, and producer Jack Warner wouldn't consider the unknown Andrews for the movie.

"Wouldn't it be loverly?"

Rex Harrison played Henry Higgins, professor of phonetics, on stage and on screen, to great acclaim. Higgins undertakes to transform Cockney London flower girl Eliza into a lady, by teaching her to speak English "properly," so that even royalty would be fooled.

Top: The makeup department decreed that Audrey's face was too square and her head too flat. They compensated with a rounded bouffant hairstyle for Eliza's flower girl persona. Audrey said that she really wanted to look beautiful in *My Fair Lady*. She was transformed in this glorious, Cecil Beaton-designed gown.

Opposite: Audrey had always looked good in hats, from ingénue Gigi's boater to this masterly Beaton confection.

Bottom: Audrey arrived extra early on set, as the makeup for the Covent Garden scenes took hours to achieve. The makeup artists rubbed Vaseline and dirt into her hair and grit under her fingernails and in her ears.

As soon as Audrey accepted the role of Eliza she began intensive coaching in speech and singing. The Cockney accent was very difficult, and she was determined to sing all her own songs. In the event, the studio chose Marni Nixon to overdub all but one ("Just You Wait") of the Lerner and Loewe songs.

Just you wait

Audrey was bitterly disappointed, and many people believed that this—and the fact that Julie Andrews, with her magnificent voice, had been passed over for the role—robbed Audrey of an Oscar for *My Fair Lady*. The Academy awarded it to Julie Andrews in her first movie, *Mary Poppins*.

Opposite: This studio portrait celebrates the splendor of Cecil Beaton's Edwardian costumes for *My Fair Lady* and subtly reflects the emergence of "Op art" in the 1960s.

Below: Audrey seems hardly changed in a decade in this exquisite portrait. But her early privations and private tragedies had taken their toll on her health. She found it impossible to gain weight and lost 8 lb/3.5 kg or more during the course of filming.

How to Steal a Million

It was 1966 and for the third time Wyler, the tough director, and Audrey, the fragile beauty he had discovered, had made another movie together: a jolly crime caper and romance, entitled, in the spirit of the self-help sixties, *How to Steal a Million*. For the first time, she had a leading man nearer her own age in Peter O'Toole, three years her junior.

Cast in stone

She is Nicole, daughter of Charles, an art forger. He is Simon, an investigator into the provenance of Charles's work. When they fall in love they conspire to steal a forged sculpture to save Charles from discovery. Together the stars giggled their way through shooting and enjoyed and loved one another's work.

Top: Even masked, no one could fail to recognize Audrey's radiant complexion and beautiful bone structure. *How to Steal a Million* was partly shot in Paris, and Audrey was able to fly home to Mel and their son, Sean, at weekends. Mel's absence from the set gave rise to rumors that their marriage was fragile.

Bottom: A wistful Nicole considers her options. Audrey's geometric haircut was the epitome of 1960s chic.

Opposite: Only Audrey Hepburn or a fashion model could have made this high fashion 1960s "crash helmet" hat and goggle sunglasses look chic rather than absurd.

Two for the Road

Two for the Road, released in 1967, was directed by Stanley Donen with an innovative screenplay by Frederic Raphael, and starred Albert Finney (seven years Audrey's junior!) as architect Mark Wallace, and Audrey as his wife Joanna. It is a comic, dramatic analysis of their twelve-year marriage, in nonsequential scenes, each set on a different road trip through France. Luxury cars are a major part of the supporting cast, with a hit theme tune by Henry Mancini.

Beauty before age

Audrey's part calls for her to play a twenty-year-old and a woman in her early thirties, which, nearing forty, she does effortlessly. Audrey and Finney embarked on a passionate affair during the filming.

Right: Audrey's look kept subtle pace with the times, without altering her fundamental style and elegance, though her eyebrows became finer, movie by movie. For the first time she was not dressed by Givenchy.

Left: In the optimistic spirit of the times the tagline of this poster reads, "They make something wonderful out of being alive!"

Opposite: Joanna and Mark looking forward to their future. Ever the professional, Audrey looked ravishing in this demanding role despite suffering a recent, heartbreaking miscarriage before shooting began.

Wait Until Dark

Back in Hollywood, Audrey's next film, a tense thriller, *Wait Until Dark* (1967), was produced by Mel Ferrer and directed by Terence Young. The plot centers on a blind woman, Susy (Hepburn) whose photographer husband, Sam (Efrem Zimbalist Jr.) unknowingly brings a drug-filled doll into their apartment. Alone in the flat, Susy is terrorized by the villains, led by Alan Arkin, in their attempts to retrieve it.

Helplessness and strength

Audrey's performance is a tour de force, calling upon all her talent and training as an actor to convey helplessness and strength in equal measure. She attended a school for the blind to inform her performance, rather than call upon a white stick and dark glasses to convey her blindness. She was breathtakingly successful.

Left: With meticulous preparation, Audrey conveyed blindness with just her eyes and body language.

Opposite: *Wait until Dark* was to be Audrey Hepburn's penultimate major motion picture and, as this image shows, it was a bravura performance. Audrey is in virtually every scene and maintains the tension and subtlety of her performance throughout. As she said herself, she acted from the inside out. While in her private life her marriage collapsed, she remained the consummate professional. After filming ended Audrey suffered yet another miscarriage—aged thirty-eight. And on the day of the press screening her impending divorce was announced.

Robin and Marian

In 1967, heartbroken, physically and emotionally exhausted, Audrey went into virtual retirement. At the end of the sixties, she met and married Italian doctor Andrea Dotti and, in 1970, her second child, Luca Dotti, was born. And, at last, she returned to the screen to costar with Sean Connery in Richard Lester's *Robin and Marian* (1976).

In the greenwood

This unusual interpretation of the legend of Robin Hood features an older Robin (Connery), returned from service to King Richard, and his reunion with, and rescue of, an older Lady Marian (Hepburn), now an abbess, still threatened by the wicked Sheriff of Nottingham. This was a touching and imaginative movie, and Audrey's performance had lost nothing of its subtlety, nuance, and skill. She was, of course, beautiful still.

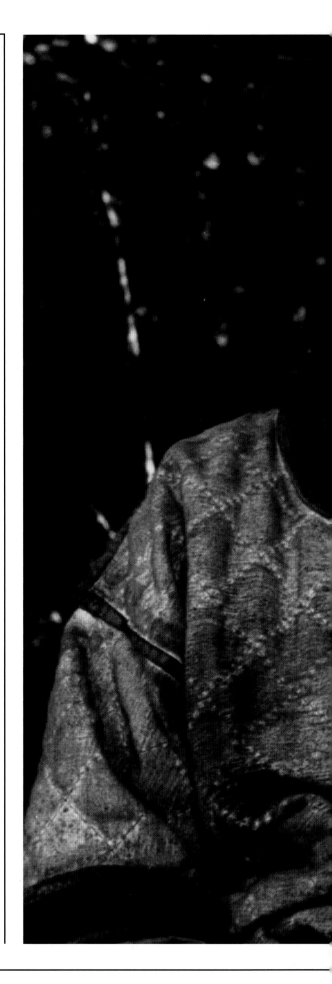

Right: A moment of peace for Sean Connery and Audrey Hepburn as Robin and Marian, outlaws to the end. Robin and Marian's tempestuous relationship is as volatile as ever, but tempered by experience, and Connery and Hepburn interpret their roles with their own wisdom of maturity.

Portraits — 1960s

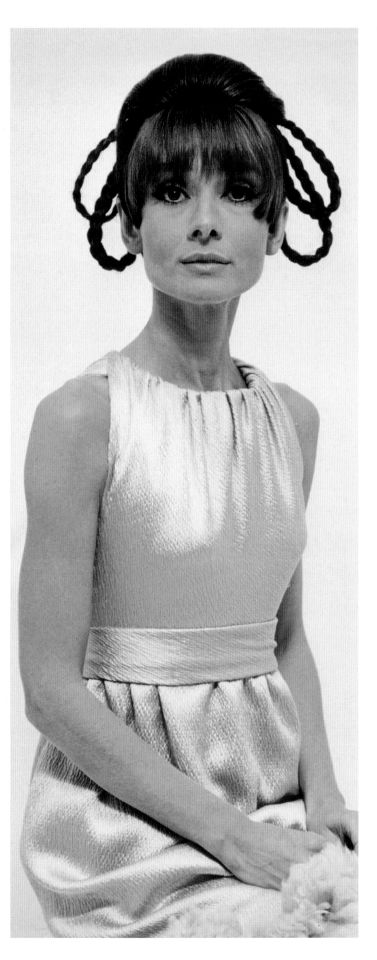

Opposite: This studio still from 1963 shows Audrey in a pensive mood, yet the young actress who became a star a decade before still conveys her unique combination of strength and fragility, intelligence and grace, now with something of the joys and sadness of her private life in her eyes. Also featured: *the* classic 1960s wicker chair and perhaps a hint of a Beatles haircut.

Left: A very different look for Audrey Hepburn, this studio portrait was taken during the making of *Two for the Road* (1967). Her husband, Mel Ferrer, had persuaded her, in this and her next movie, *Wait until Dark*, to abandon the elegant simplicity of her Givenchy wardrobe for ready-to-wear clothes. He resented her friendship with Givenchy, whom he suspected of exploiting Audrey, notably in her sponsorship of Givenchy's fragrance, without payment. Audrey was steadfast in her loyalty to Givenchy, while attempting to maintain her marriage.

They All Laughed

Peter Bogdanovich directed *They All Laughed* (1981) starring Audrey Hepburn as Angela Niotes, the elegant wife of an Italian industrialist, and Ben Gazzara as private eye John Russo. This complicated romantic comedy, set in New York, is the saga of three detectives trailing two beautiful women suspected of infidelity by their husbands; but the detectives become romantically involved with their subjects, and the plot thickens.

Art imitating life

Allegedly, Gazzara and Hepburn were romantically involved themselves during the making of the movie, and critics have commented on their on-screen chemistry. The film is also notable for the fact that Audrey's son, Sean Ferrer, appears as the paramour of Dolores, the other subject of the investigation.

Right: Audrey Hepburn as Angela Niotes and Ben Gazzara as John Russo in *They All Laughed*. Apart from a cameo appearance in *Always*, this movie was Audrey's last.

Always

In 1989, the legendary director, Steven Spielberg, cast the legendary actress, Audrey Hepburn, in her final big screen role as an angel, Hap, in *Always*. The movie stars Richard Dreyfuss as a daredevil pilot and Holly Hunter as the woman who loves and loses him; but does she …?

Angel

Audrey ends her screen career as she began it: an incandescent, beautiful woman and a fine actress working with a great director, albeit in a cameo role. The movie is lent greater poignancy as Audrey had only a short time to live. The rest of her life was devoted to her work as an ambassador for UNICEF. Audrey Hepburn died on January 20, 1993, aged sixty-three.

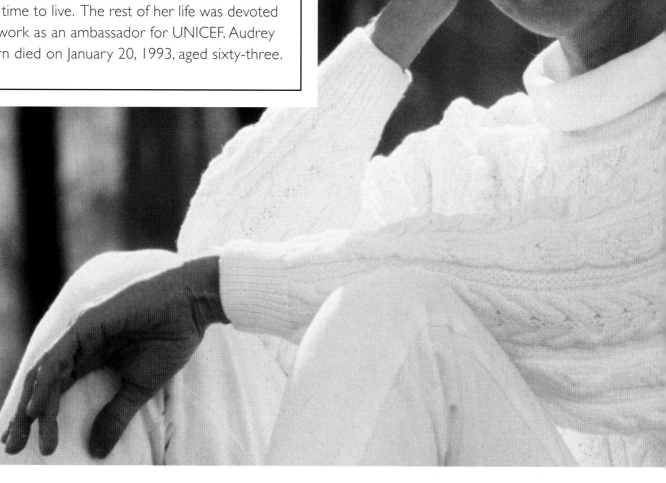

Goodwill
Ambassador

"I can testify to what UNICEF means to children, because I was among those who received food and medical relief right after World War II," said actress Audrey Hepburn on her appointment as a Goodwill Ambassador in 1989. "I have a long-lasting gratitude and trust for what UNICEF does."

Audrey was as committed to her work for the world's poorest children as she had been to everything that she had engaged in during her career and personal relationships. She received the Presidential Medal of Freedom in 1992. She undertook many missions for the organization, beginning with her first to war-torn and famine-stricken Ethiopia soon after her appointment, and including: a polio vaccine project in Turkey, a women's training program in Venezuela, the rescue of street children in Guatemala and Honduras, a radio literacy program in El Salvador, school inspections in Bangladesh, projects for impoverished children in Thailand, nutrition projects in Vietnam, and camps for displaced children in Sudan. She also raised funds and lobbied governments as well as promoting the work of UNICEF. She continued her work until her death.

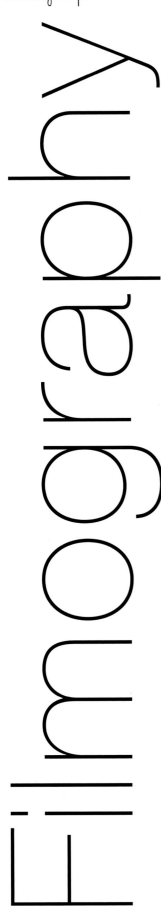

Nederlands in 7 Lessen (1948)

One Wild Oat (1951)

Laughter in Paradise (1951)

The Lavender Hill Mob (1951)

Young Wives' Tale (1951)

Secret People (1952)

Monte Carlo Baby (1952)

Roman Holiday (1953)

Sabrina (1954)

War and Peace (1956)

Funny Face (1957)

Love in the Afternoon (1957)

Green Mansions (1959)

The Nun's Story (1959)

The Unforgiven (1960)

Breakfast at Tiffany's (1961)

The Children's Hour (1961)

Charade (1963)

Paris When It Sizzles (1964)

My Fair Lady (1964)

How to Steal a Million (1966)

Two for the Road (1967)

Wait Until Dark (1967)

Robin and Marian (1976)

Bloodline (1979)

They All Laughed (1981)

Always (1989)

Academy Awards, U.S.A.

1993	Won	Jean Hersholt Humanitarian Award (The award, which was voted prior to her death, was presented posthumously).	
1968	Nominated	Oscar	Best Actress in a Leading Role *Wait Until Dark* (1967)
1962	Nominated	Oscar	Best Actress in a Leading Role *Breakfast at Tiffany's* (1961)
1960	Nominated	Oscar	Best Actress in a Leading Role *The Nun's Story* (1959)
1955	Nominated	Oscar	Best Actress in a Leading Role *Sabrina* (1954)
1954	Won	Oscar	Best Actress in a Leading Role *Roman Holiday* (1953)

Golden Globes, U.S.A.

1990	Won	Cecil B. DeMille Award
1968	Nominated	Golden Globe Best Motion Picture Actress—Drama *Wait Until Dark* (1967)
	Nominated	Golden Globe Best Motion Picture Actress—Musical/Comedy *Two for the Road* (1967)
1965	Nominated	Golden Globe Best Motion Picture Actress—Musical/Comedy *My Fair Lady* (1964)
1964	Nominated	Golden Globe Best Motion Picture Actress—Musical/Comedy *Charade* (1963)
1962	Nominated	Golden Globe Best Motion Picture Actress—Musical/Comedy *Breakfast at Tiffany's* (1961)
1960	Nominated	Golden Globe Best Motion Picture Actress—Drama *The Nun's Story* (1959)
1958	Nominated	Golden Globe Best Motion Picture Actress—Musical/Comedy *Love in the Afternoon* (1957)
1957	Nominated	Golden Globe Best Motion Picture Actress—Drama *War and Peace* (1956)
1955	Won	Henrietta Award World Film Favorite—Female
1954	Won	Golden Globe Best Motion Picture Actress—Drama *Roman Holiday* (1953)

BAFTA Awards

1965	Won	BAFTA Film Award Best British Actress *Charade* (1963)
1960	Won	BAFTA Film Award Best British Actress *The Nun's Story* (1959) U.S.A.
1957	Nominated	BAFTA Film Award Best British Actress *War and Peace* (1956) Italy/U.S.A.
1955	Nominated	BAFTA Film Award Best British Actress *Sabrina* (1954) U.S.A.
1954	Won	BAFTA Film Award Best British Actress *Roman Holiday* (1953) U.S.A.

Images from

THE KOBAL COLLECTION